WORDS TO
COMFORT

WORDS TO
HEAL

WORDS TO
COMFORT
WORDS TO
HEAL

Poems and Meditations for those who Grieve

COMPILED BY JULIET MABEY

ONEWORLD

OXFORD

WORDS TO COMFORT, WORDS TO HEAL

Oneworld Publications
(Sales and Editorial)
185 Banbury Road
Oxford OX2 7AR
England
www.oneworld-publications.com

ISBN 1–85168–154–X

Cover and text design by Design Deluxe
Printed in China by Sun Fung Offset Binding Co. Ltd

CONTENTS

PREFACE

GRIEF IS AN intensely personal experience. Just as every individual and every relationship is unique, so each person's reaction to the loss of a loved one – or to the imminence of their own death – is different. Our response to death is intricately interwoven with our sense of who we are and how we see our place in the scheme of things, with our ideas about the purpose of life and the meaning of death, our relationships with others and, for many, with an ultimate power, God.

Yet while each one of us has our own unique grief, there are common themes within the variety of human responses to death. We may find in the sharing of another's grief words that offer true comfort, images that help us come to terms with our loss, or advice that makes our own grief easier to bear.

Many of the poems and writings chosen for this anthology are time-honoured favourites by well-known writers that men and women have turned to through the ages and around the world. Some express fear, despair, anger and deep sorrow, resonating with the heartache of regret and the agony of loss. Others offer a celebration of a life that brought great joy to those who were touched by it and share the confidence of a love that continues beyond the separation of death. While some are achingly personal, others focus on the universal themes of life, death and the human sense of purpose in this world.

Together they explore the diversity of grief – from the loss of a partner or child to the meaning of life, from the mystery of death to the comfort of a life beyond, from the celebration of a life well lived to embarking on a positive future without a loved one.

As we share the grief of the writers of these extracts, they reach out and touch us with their hearts and lives, and even if it is just for a short moment, we know that we are not alone. Whether you are facing your own death or coming to terms with the loss of a loved one, or you know someone who is and don't know how to help, this little anthology of poetry and prose, drawn from the richness of the world's cultural and religious heritage, will offer solace and support.

JULIET MABEY

A TIME
TO GRIEVE

Give sorrow words. The grief that does not speak
Whispers the o'erfraught heart, and bids it break.

WILLIAM SHAKESPEARE

NO ONE ever told me that grief felt so like fear. I am not afraid, but the sensation is like being afraid. The same fluttering in the stomach, the same restlessness, the yawning. I keep on swallowing.

At other times it feels like being mildly drunk, or concussed. There is a sort of invisible blanket between the world and me. I find it hard to take in what anyone says. Or perhaps, hard to want to take it in. It is so uninteresting. Yet I want the others to be about me. I dread the moments when the house is empty. If only they would talk to one another and not to me . . .

An odd by-product of my loss is that I'm afraid of being an embarrassment to everyone I meet. At work, at the club, in the street, I see people, as they approach me, trying to make up their minds whether they'll 'say something about it' or not. I hate it if they do, and if they don't . . .

And grief still feels like fear. Perhaps more strictly, like suspense. Or like waiting; just hanging about waiting for something to happen. It gives life a permanently provisional feeling. It doesn't seem worth starting anything. I can't settle down. I yawn, I fidget, I smoke too much. Up till this I always had too little time. Now there is nothing but time. Almost pure time, empty successiveness . . .

C. S. LEWIS, *from* A GRIEF OBSERVED

No Worst, There is None

NO WORST, there is none. Pitched past pitch of grief,
More pangs will, schooled at forepangs, wilder wring.
Comforter, where, where is your comforting?
Mary, mother of us, where is your relief?
My cries heave, herds-long; huddle in a main, a chief
Woe, world-sorrow; on an age-old anvil wince and sing–
Then lull, then leave off. Fury had shrieked 'No ling-
ering! Let me be fell: force I must be brief'.

O the mind, mind has mountains; cliffs of fall
Frightful, sheer, no-man-fathomed. Hold them cheap
May who ne'er hung there. Nor does long our small
Durance deal with that steep or deep. Here! creep,
Wretch, under a comfort serves in a whirlwind: all
Life does end and each day dies with sleep.

GERARD MANLEY HOPKINS

ON THE DEATH OF HIS FATHER

I LOOK up and see his curtains and bed;
I look down and examine his table and mat.
The things are there just as before;
But the man they belonged to is not there
His spirit suddenly has taken flight
And left me behind far away.
To whom shall I look, on whom rely?
My tears flow in an endless stream . . .
I alone am desolate
Dreading the days of our long parting;
My grieving heart's settled pain
No one else can understand.
There is a saying among people
'Sorrow makes us grow old.'
Alas, alas for my white hairs!
All too early they have come!
Long wailing, long sighing
My thoughts are fixed on my sage parent.
They say the good live long;
Then why was he not spared?

WEI WÊN-TI, *from* CHINESE POEMS
Translated by ARTHUR WALEY

STOP ALL the clocks, cut off the telephone,
Prevent the dog from barking with a juicy bone,
Silence the pianos and with muffled drum
Bring out the coffin, let the mourners come.

Let aeroplanes circle moaning overhead
Scribbling on the sky the message He is Dead,
Put crêpe bows round the white necks of the public doves,
Let the traffic policemen wear black cotton gloves.

He was my North, my South, my East and West,
My working week and my Sunday rest,
My noon, my midnight, my talk, my song;
I thought that love would last for ever: I was wrong.

The stars are not wanted now; put out every one:
Pack up the moon and dismantle the sun;
Pour away the ocean and sweep up the woods:
For nothing now can ever come to any good.

W. H. AUDEN, *from* TWELVE SONGS

PAIN

AND A woman spoke, saying, Tell us of Pain. And he said:
Your pain is the breaking of the shell that encloses your
   understanding.
Even as the stone of the fruit must break, that its heart may
   stand in the sun, so must you know pain.
And could you keep your heart in wonder at the daily miracles of
   your life, your pain would not seem less wondrous than your joy;
And you would accept the seasons of your heart, even as you
   have always accepted the seasons that pass over your fields.
And you would watch with serenity through the winters of
   your grief.
Much of your pain is self-chosen.
It is the bitter potion by which the physician within you heals
   your sick self.
Therefore trust the physician and drink his remedy in silence
   and tranquillity:
For his hand, though heavy and hard, is guided by the tender
   hand of the Unseen.
And the cup he brings, though it burn your lips, has been
   fashioned of the clay which the Potter has moistened with
   His own sacred tears.

KAHLIL GIBRAN, *from* THE PROPHET

MY DARLING, thou wilt never know
The grinding agony of woe
    As we have borne for thee.
Thus may we consolation tear
E'en from the depth of our despair
    And wasting misery . . .

Nor knew'st thou what it is to lie
Beholding forth with tear dimmed eye
    Life's lone wilderness.
'Weary, weary, dark and drear,
How shall I the journey bear,
    The burden and distress?'

Then since thou art spared such pain
We will not wish thee here again
    He that lives must mourn
God relieve us through our misery
And give us rest and joy with thee
    When we reach our bourne!

CHARLOTTE BRONTË

DEATH SETS a thing significant
The eye had hurried by
Except a perished Creature
Entreat us tenderly

To ponder little workmanships
In crayon, or in wool,
With 'This was last her fingers did' –
Industrious until

The thimble weighed too heavy,
The stitches stopped themselves,
And then 'twas put among the dust
Upon the closet shelves.

A book I have, a friend gave,
Whose pencil, here and there,
Had notched the place that pleased him,
At rest his fingers are.

Now, when I read, I read not,
For interrupting tears
Obliterate the etchings
Too costly for repairs.

EMILY DICKINSON

WORDS ABOUT GRIEF

GRIEF CAN return without warning. It's
    Seldom cemeteries
Or news of other deaths that my grief fits
But places of great beauty where I was,

However briefly, happy with the one
    I loved who died. I know
Many feel happier when again they've gone
To such a place with grief. One thing I do

Know is that after years grief brings a pang
    As terrible almost
As that first rending. Death, where love's been strong,
Can always make you feel entirely lost

Or so it does with me. Time does not heal,
It makes a half-stitched scar
That can be broken and you feel
Grief as total as in its first hour.

ELIZABETH JENNINGS

THE DEAD are gone and with them we cannot converse.
The living are here and ought to have our love.
Leaving the city-gate I look ahead
And see before me only mounds and tombs.
The old graves are ploughed up into fields,
The pines and cypresses are hewn for timber.
In the white aspens sad wings sing;
Their long murmuring kills my heart with grief.
I want to go home, to ride to my village gate.
I want to go back, but there's no road back.

From CHINESE POEMS
Translated by ARTHUR WALEY

GOOD GOD! how often are we to die before we go quite off
this stage? In every friend we lose a part of ourselves, and
the best part.

ALEXANDER POPE

TO EVERYTHING there is a season,
and a time to every purpose under the heaven:
a time to be born, and a time to die;
a time to plant, and a time to pluck up that which is planted;
a time to kill, and a time to heal;
a time to break down, and a time to build up;
a time to weep, and a time to laugh;
a time to mourn, and a time to dance;
a time to cast away stones, and a time to gather stones together;
a time to embrace, and a time to refrain from embracing;
a time to get, and a time to lose;
a time to keep, and a time to cast away;
a time to rend, and a time to sew;
a time to keep silence, a time to speak;
a time to love, and a time to hate;
a time of war, and a time of peace.

ECCLESIASTES 3: 1–8

THE DEPTHS of sorrow in tears have not been measured.
The mountains and the hills will pass away
Like flooded rivers and streams. Tears may flow
But what your destiny has given you must accept.
Brother, were I a teardrop I would fall like flooded waters
For the deep limits of sorrow's tears are not yet found.

TRADITIONAL ELEGY *from* THE GOND, INDIA

THE IMMORTALITY OF LOVE

Unable are the Loved to die

For love is immortality.

EMILY DICKINSON

CONTINUITIES

NOTHING IS ever really lost, or can be lost,
No birth, identity, form – no object of the world.
Nor life, nor force, nor any visible thing;
Appearance must not foil, nor shifted sphere confuse thy
    brain.
Ample are time and space – ample the fields of Nature.
The body, sluggish, aged, cold – the embers left from earlier
    fires,
The light in the eye grown dim, shall duly flame again;
The sun now low in the west rises for mornings and for noons
    continual;
To frozen clods ever the spring's invisible law returns,
With grass and flowers and summer fruits and corn.

WALT WHITMAN

WHY DO they weep for those in the silent Tomb,
Dropping their tears like grain? . . .
Love is not changed by Death,
And nothing is lost and all in the end is harvest.

EDITH SITWELL, *from* EURYDICE

PEOPLE DO not die for us immediately, but remain bathed in a sort of *aura* of life which bears no relation to true immortality but through which they continue to occupy our thoughts as when they were alive. It is as though they were travelling abroad.

MARCEL PROUST, *from* REMEMBRANCE OF THINGS PAST

HE DID not lose his place in the minds of men because he was out of their sight.

JOHN HENRY NEWMAN, *from* CATHOLIC SERMONS

SURPRISED BY joy, impatient as the wind,
I wished to share the transport – oh! with whom
But thee, long buried in the silent tomb,
That spot which no vicissitude can find?
Love, faithful love, recalled thee to my mind,
But how could I forget thee? Through what power,
Even for the least division of an hour,
Have I been so beguiled as to be blind
To my most grievous loss? That thought's return
Was the worst pang that sorrow ever bore,
Save one – one only – when I stood forlorn,
Knowing my heart's best treasure was no more:
That neither present time, nor years unborn
Could to my sight that heavenly face restore . . .
Of, if such thoughts must needs deceive,
Kind spirits! may we not believe
That they, so happy and so fair,
Through your sweet influence, and the care
Of pitying heaven, at least were free
From touch of *deadly* injury?
Destined, whate'er their earthly doom,
For mercy and immortal bloom!

WILLIAM WORDSWORTH, *from* INTIMATIONS OF IMMORTALITY

LOVE LIVES BEYOND THE TOMB

LOVE LIVES beyond the tomb
And earth, which fades like dew!
I love the fond,
The faithful, and the true.

Love lives in sleep:
'Tis happiness of healthy dreams;
Eve's dews may weep,
But love delightful seems.

'Tis seen in flowers,
And in the morning's pearly dew;
In earth's green hours,
And in the heaven's eternal blue.

'Tis heard in Spring
When light and sunbeams, warm and kind,
On angel's wing
Bring love and music to the mind . . .

JOHN CLARE

REMEMBRANCE

COLD IN the earth – and the deep snow piled above thee,
Far, far removed, cold in the dreary grave!
Have I forgot my Only Love, to love thee,
Severed at last by Time's all-severing wave?

Now, when alone, do my thoughts no longer hover
Over the mountains, on that northern shore;
Resting their wings where heath and fern-leaves cover
Thy noble heart forever, ever more?

Cold in the earth – and fifteen wild Decembers,
From those brown hills have melted into spring –
Faithful indeed is the spirit that remembers
After such years of change and suffering!

Sweet Love of youth, forgive if I forget thee
While the World's tide is bearing me along;
Other desires and other hopes beset me,
Hopes which obscure but cannot do thee wrong.

No later light has lightened up my heaven,
No second morn has ever shone for me:
All my life's bliss from thy dear life was given –
All my life's bliss is in the grave with thee.

But when the days of golden dreams had perished
And even Despair was powerless to destroy,
Then did I learn how existence could be cherished,
Strengthened and fed without the aid of joy;

Then did I check the tears of useless passion,
Weaned my young soul from yearning after thine;
Sternly denied its burning wish to hasten
Down to that tomb already more than mine.

And even yet, I dare not let it languish,
dare not indulge in Memory's rapturous pain;
Once drinking deep of that divinest anguish,
How could I seek the empty world again?

EMILY BRONTË

DEAR SIR,

I AM VERY sorry for your immense loss, which is a repetition of what all feel in this valley of misery & the happiness mixed. I know that our deceased friends are more really with us than when they were apparent to our mortal part. Thirteen years ago I lost a brother, & with his spirit I converse daily and hourly in the Spirit & See him in my remembrance, in the regions of my Imagination. I hear his advice & even now write from his Dictate. Forgive me for Expressing to you my Enthusiasm which I wish all to partake of Since it is to me a Source of Immortal Joy: even in this world by it I am the companion of Angels. May you continue to be so more & more & to be more & more persuaded that every Mortal loss is an Immortal Gain. The Ruins of Time build Mansions in Eternity . . .

   . . . feeling heartily your grief with a brother's Sympathy.

I remain, Dear Sir, Your humble Servant

WILLIAM BLAKE
Lambeth, May 6 1800

THEY TOLD me, Heraclitus, they told me you were dead,
They brought me bitter news to hear and bitter tears to shed.
I wept as I remembered how often you and I
Had tired the sun with talking and sent him down the sky.

And now that thou art lying, my dear old Carian guest,
A handful of grey ashes, long, long ago at rest,
Still are thy pleasant voices, thy nightingales, awake;
For Death, he taketh all away, but them he cannot take.

CALLIMACHUS, *from* IONICUS

JEWELS IN MY HAND

I HOLD dead friends like jewels in my hand
Watching their brilliance gleam against my palm
Turquoise and emerald, jade, a golden band

All ravages of time they can withstand
Like talismans their grace keeps me from harm
I hold dead friends like jewels in my hand

I see them standing in some borderland
Their hands half-turned, waiting to take my arm
Turquoise and emerald, jade, a golden band

I'm not afraid they will misunderstand
My turning to them like a magic charm
I hold dead friends like jewels in my hand
Turquoise and emerald, jade, a golden band.

SASHA MOORSOM

Sonnet XLIII

HOW DO I love thee? – Let me count the ways!
I love thee to the depth & breadth & height
My soul can reach, when feeling out of sight
For the ends of Being and Ideal Grace.
I love thee to the level of everyday's
Most quiet need, by sun & candlelight.
I love thee freely, as men strive for Right, –
I love thee purely, as they turn from Praise,!
I love thee with the passion, put to use
In my old griefs, . . and with my childhood's faith! –
I love thee with the love I seemed to lose
With my lost Saints! – I love thee with the breath,
Smiles, tears, of all my life! – and, if God choose,
I shall but love thee better after death.

ELIZABETH BARRETT BROWNING

THEY SHALL grow not old, as we that are left grow old:
Age shall not weary them, nor the years condemn.
At the going down of the sun and in the morning
We will remember them . . .

As the stars that shall be bright when we are dust,
Moving in marches upon the heavenly plain,
As the stars that are starry in the time of our darkness,
To the end, to the end, they remain.

LAWRENCE BINYON, *from* FOR THE FALLEN (SEPTEMBER 1914)

LOSING A PARTNER

Grief is not forever – but love is.

ANON

DEATH IS nothing at all . . . It does not count. I have only slipped away into the next room. Nothing has happened. Everything remains exactly as it was. I am I, and you are you, and the old life we lived so fondly together is untouched, unchanged. Whatever we were to each other, that we are still. Call me by the old familiar name. Speak of me in the easy way which you always used. Put no difference into your tone. Wear no forced air of solemnity of sorrow. Laugh as we always laughed at the little jokes that we enjoyed together. Play, smile, think of me, pray for me. Let my name be ever the household word that it always was. Life means all that it ever meant. It is the same as it ever was. There is absolute and unbroken continuity. What is this death but a negligible accident? Why should I be out of mind because I am out of sight? I am waiting for you, for an interval, somewhere very near, just round the corner. All is well. Nothing is hurt; nothing is lost. One brief moment and all will be as it was before. How we shall laugh at the trouble of parting when we meet again!

HENRY SCOTT HOLLAND, *from* FIBRES OF FAITH

MY LOVE is like a red red rose
  That's newly sprung in June:
My love is like the melodie
  That's sweetly play'd in tune.

As fair thou, my bonnie lass,
  So deep in love am I;
And I will love thee still, my dear,
  Till a' the seas gang dry.

Till a' the seas gang dry, my dear,
  And the rocks melt wi' the sun:
And I will love thee still, my dear,
  While the sands o' life shall run.

And fare thee weel, my only love,
  And fare thee weel a while!
And I will come again, my love,
  Tho' it were ten thousand mile.

ROBERT BURNS

SLEEP ON my *Love* in thy cold bed
Never to be disquieted!
My last good night! Thou wilt not wake
Till I thy fate shall overtake:
Till age, or grief, or sickness must
Marry my body to that dust
It so much loves; and fill the room
My heart keeps empty in thy Tomb.
Stay for me there; I will not fail
To meet thee in that hollow Vale.
And think not much of my delay;
I am already on the way,
And follow thee with all the speed
Desire can make, or sorrows breed.
Each minute is a short degree,
And every hour a step towards thee.
At night when I betake to rest,
Next morn I rise nearer my West
Of life, almost by eight hours' sail,
Than when sleep breath'd his drowsy gale.
    Thus from the Sun my Bottom steers,
And my days' Compass downward bears:
Nor labour I to stem the tide
Through which to *Thee* I swiftly glide.

'Tis true, with shame and grief I yield,
Thou like the *Vann* first took'st the field,
And gotten hast the victory
In thus adventuring to die
Before me, whose more years might crave
A just precedence in the grave.
But hark! My pulse like a soft Drum
Beats my approach, tells *Thee* I come;
And slow howe'er my marches be,
I shall at last sit down by *Thee*
    The thought of this bids me go on,
And wait my dissolution
With hope and comfort. *Dear* (forgive
The crime) I am content to live
Divided, but with half a heart,
Till we shall meet and never part.

HENRY KING, *from* THE EXEQUY

AND THEN one or other dies. And we think of this as love cut short; like a dance stepped in mid career or a flower with its head unluckily snapped off – something truncated and therefore, lacking its due shape. I wonder. If, as I can't help suspecting, the dead also feel the pains of separation (and this may be one of their purgatorial sufferings), then for both lovers, and for all pairs of lovers without exception, bereavement is a universal and integral part of our experience of love. It follows marriage as normally as marriage follows courtship or as autumn follows summer. It is not a truncation of the process but one of its phases; not the interruption of the dance, but the next figure. We are 'taken out of ourselves' by the loved one while she is here. Then comes the tragic figure of the dance in which we must learn to be still taken out of ourselves though the bodily presence is withdrawn, to love the very Her, and not fall back to loving our past, or our memory, or our sorrow, or our relief from sorrow, or our own love.

C. S. LEWIS, *from* A GRIEF OBSERVED

SONNET CXVI

LET ME not to the marriage of true minds
Admit impediments. Love is not love
Which alters when it alteration finds,
Or bends with the remover to remove:
O no; it is an ever fixed mark
That looks on tempests, and is never shaken;
It is the star to every wandering bark,
Whose worth's unknown, although his height be taken.
Love's not Time's fool, though rosy lips and cheeks
Within his bending sickle's compass come;
Love alters not with his brief hours and weeks,
But bears it out even to the edge of doom.
    If this be error and upon me prov'd,
    I never writ, nor no man ever lov'd.

WILLIAM SHAKESPEARE

YOU TOUCHED my life
And turned my heart around.
It seems when I found you
It was me I really found.
You opened my eyes
And now my soul can see
Our moments may be over,
Of just you here with me.

Love lives on beyond Goodbye
The truth of us will never die.
Our spirits will shine
Long after we've gone,
And so our love lives on.

There was so much
I didn't understand
When you brought me here
Far from where we all began.
The changes you made
To my life will never end.
I'll look across the distance
And know I have a friend.

Love lives on beyond Goodbye
The truth of us will never die.
Our spirits will shine
Long after we've gone,
And so our love lives on.

And so our love lives on.

ANON

AS VIRTUOUS men pass mildly away,
  And whisper to their souls to go,
Whilst some of their sad friends do say
  'The breath goes now,' and some say, 'No':

So let us melt, and make no noise,
  No tear-floods, nor sigh-tempests move,
'Twere profanation of our joys
  To tell the laity our love.

Moving of the earth brings harms and fears,
  Men reckon what it did and meant;
But trepidation of the spheres,
  Though greater far, is innocent.

Dull sublunary lovers' love
  (Whose soul is sense) cannot admit
Absence, because it doth remove
  Those things which elemented it.

But we by a love, so much refin'd,
  That ourselves know not what it is,
Inter-assurèd of the mind,
  Care less, eyes, lips, and hands to miss.

Our two souls therefore, which are one,
  Though I must go, endure not yet
A breach, but an expansion,
  Like gold to airy thinness beat.

If they be two, they are two so
  As stiff twin compasses are two,
Thy soul the fixed foot, makes no show
  To move, but doth, if th'other do.

And though it in the centre sit,
  Yet when the other far doth roam
It leans, and hearkens after it,
  And grows erect, as that comes home.

Such wilt thou be to me, who must
  Like th'other foot, obliquely run;
Thy firmness makes my circle just,
And makes me end, where I begun.

JOHN DONNE

THOUGH I am old with wandering
Through hollow lands and hilly lands,
I will find out where she has gone,
And kiss her lips and take her hands;
And walk among long dappled grass,
And pluck till time and times are done
The silver apples of the moon,
The golden apples of the sun.

W. B. YEATS, *from* THE SONG OF THE WANDERING AENGUS

FOR ONE SO YOUNG

Grieve not that I die young. Is it not well

To pass away ere life hath lost its brightness?

LADY FLORA HASTINGS

In Memory of My Dear Grandchild Elizabeth . . .

FAREWELL DEAR babe, my heart's too much content,
Farewell sweet babe, the pleasure of mine eye,
Farewell fair flower that for a space was lent,
Then ta'en away unto Eternity.
Blest babe, why should I once bewail thy fate,
Or sigh thy days so soon were terminate,
Sith thou art settled in an Everlasting state?

By nature Trees do rot when they are grown,
And Plumbs and Apples throughly ripe do fall,
And corn and grass are in their season mown,
And time brings down what is both strong and tall.
But plants new set to be eradicate,
And buds new blown, to have so short a date,
Is by his hand along that guides nature and fate.

ANNE BRADSTREET

IT IS not growing like a tree
　　In bulk, doth make Man better be;
Or standing long an oak, three hundred year,
To fall a log at last, dry, bald, and sere:
　　　　A lily of a day
　　　　Is fairer far in May,
Although it fall and die that night;
It was the plant and flower of Light.
In small proportions we just beauties see;
And in short measures life may perfect be.

BEN JONSON

NO MAN dies before his hour. The time you leave behind was no more yours, than that which was before your birth, and concerneth you no more.

MICHEL DE MONTAIGNE, *from* ESSAIS

MORTAL MAN, you have been a citizen in this great City; what does it matter to you whether for five or fifty years? For what is according to its law is equal for every man. Why is it hard, then, if Nature who brought you in, and no despot nor unjust judge, sends you out of the City – as though the master of the show, who engaged an actor, were to dismiss him from the stage? 'But I have not spoken my five acts, only three.' 'What you say is true, but in life three acts are the whole play.' For He determines the perfect whole, the cause yesterday of your composition, today of your dissolution; you are the cause of neither. Leave the stage, therefore, and be reconciled, for He also who lets his servant depart is reconciled.

MARCUS AURELIUS, *from* MEDITATIONS
Translated by A. S. L. FARQUHARSON

'LISTEN, MOTHER,' said Father Zossima. 'Once in olden times a holy saint saw in the Temple a mother like you weeping for her little one, her only one, whom God had taken. "Knowest thou not," said the saint to her, "how bold these little ones are before the throne of God? Verily, there are none bolder than they in the Kingdom of Heaven. 'Thou didst give us life, oh Lord,' they say, 'and scarcely had we looked upon it when Thou didst take it back again.' And so boldly they ask and ask again that God gives them at once the rank of angels . . ." That's what the saint said to the weeping mother of old. He was a great saint and he could not have spoken falsely.'

DOSTOEVSKY, *from* THE BROTHERS KARAMAZOV

HE DID but float a little way
Adown the stream of time;
With dreamy eyes catching the ripples play,
Or listening their fairy chime.
His slender sail
Ne'er felt the gale;
He did but float a little way,
And, putting to the shore
While yet 'twas early day,
Went calmly on his way,
To dwell with us no more!
No jarring did he feel,
No grating on his vessel's keel;
A strip of yellow sand
Mingled the waters with the land,
Where he was seen no more:
O stern word – nevermore!
Full short his journey was; no dust
Of earth into his sandals clave;
The weary weight that old men must,
He bore not to the grave.

He seemed a cherub who had lost his way
And wandered hither, so his stay
With us was short, and 'twas most meet
That he would be no delve in earth's clod,
Nor need to pause and cleanse his feet
To stand before his god:
O blest word – evermore!

JAMES RUSSELL LOWELL

FOR A CHILD BORN DEAD

WHAT CEREMONY can we fit
You into now? If you had come
Out of a warm and noisy room
To this, there'd be an opposite
For us to know you by. We could
Imagine you in lively mood

And then look at the other side,
The mood drawn out of you, the breath
Defeated by the power of death.
But we have never seen you stride
Ambitiously the world we know.
You could not come and yet you go.

But there is nothing now to mar
Your clear refusal of our world.
Not in our memories can we mould
You or distort your character.
Then all our consolation is
That grief can be as pure as this.

ELIZABETH JENNINGS

BEWAIL NOT much, my parents! me, the prey
Of ruthless Hades, and sepulchred here.
An infant, in my fifth scarce finished year,
He found all sportive, innocent, and gay,
Your young Callimachus; and if I knew
Not many joys, my griefs also were few.

LUCIAN

DOOMED TO know not Winter; only Spring – a being
Trod the flowery April blithely for a while;
Took his fill of music, joy of thought and seeing,
Came and stayed and went; nor ever ceased to smile.

Came and stayed and went; and now, when all is finished,
You alone have crossed the melancholy stream.
Yours the pang; but his, oh his, the undiminished
Undecaying gladness, undeparted dream.

R. L. STEVENSON

Upon a child that dyed

HERE SHE lies, a pretty bud,
Lately made of flesh and blood:
Who, as soon, fell fast asleep,
As her little eyes did peep.
Give her strewings; but not stir
The earth, that lightly covers her.

R. Herrick

WHAT IS THIS LIFE?

Death puts Life into perspective.

RALPH WALDO EMERSON

S O FAR as in us lies, we must play the immortal and do all in our power to live by the best element in our nature.

ARISTOTLE

I WOULD KNOW whether after the parting of the body and the soul I shall ever know more than I now know of all that which I have long wished to know; for I cannot find anything better in man than that he know, and nothing worse than that he be ignorant.

ALFRED THE GREAT

THIS LIFE is only a prelude to eternity. For that which we call death is but a pause, in truth a progress into life.

SENECA

THERE IS time of weeping and there is time of laughing. But as you see, he setteth the weeping time before, for that is the time of this wretched world and the laughing time shall come after in heaven. There is also a time of sowing, and a time of reaping too. Now must we in this world sow, that we may in the other world reap: and in this short sowing time of this weeping world, must we water our seed with the showers of our tears, and then shall we have in heaven a merry laughing harvest for ever.

SIR THOMAS MORE

THOSE FOR whom the belief in immortality is most vivid are the most likely to practice the virtues which have a survival value and the least likely to deviate into either those virtues or those vices which are exclusively human. But, as skepticism grows, the pattern of human conduct inevitably changes. The demand that life justify itself can no longer be postponed, and hence there begins the search for values which shall have meaning for the individual consciousness as opposed to those which have meaning only for Nature and her inscrutable appetite for mere life in itself. The simpler man, caught in a meaningless but exacting round of duties, does no more than fall into that 'quiet desperation' . . . But minds which are keener and wills which are stronger than the average do not rest in 'quiet desperation' palliated by illusion. They demand of life some meaning comprehensible to them, and they set themselves up against Nature because they have come to realize that her values are not for them and her contentment not theirs.

JOSEPH WOOD KRUTCH, *from* THE MODERN TEMPER

LIFE

I MADE a posy, while the day ran by:
Here will I smell my remnant out, and tie
  My life within this band.
But time did beckon to the flowers, and they
By noon most cunningly did steal away,
  And wither'd in my hand.

My hand was next to them, and then my heart:
I took, without more thinking, in good part
  Time's gentle admonition:
Who did so sweetly death's sad taste convey,
Making my mind to smell my fatal day;
  Yet sugring the suspicion.

Farewell dear flowers, sweetly your time ye spent,
Fit, while ye liv'd, for smell or ornament,
  And after death for cures.
I follow straight without complaints or grief,
Since if my scent be good, I care not, if
  It be as short as yours.

GEORGE HERBERT

IN A harbour, two ships sailed: one setting forth on a voyage, the other coming home to port. Everyone cheered the ship going out, but the ship sailing in was scarcely noticed. To this, a wise man said: 'Do not rejoice over a ship setting out to sea, for you cannot know what terrible storms it may encounter and what fearful dangers it may have to endure. Rejoice rather over the ship that has safely reached port and brings its passengers home in peace.'

And this is the way of the world: When a child is born, all rejoice; when someone dies, all weep. We should do the opposite. For no one can tell what trials and travails await a newborn child; but when a mortal dies in peace, we should rejoice, for he has completed a long journey, and there is no greater boon than to leave this world with the imperishable crown of a good name.

From THE TALMUD

HAPPY THE man, and happy he alone,
 He who can call today his own:
 He who, secure within, can say,
Tomorrow do thy worst, for I have lived today.
 Be fair or foul or rain or shine
The joys I have possessed, in spite of fate, are mine.
Not Heaven itself upon the past has power,
But what has been, has been, and I have had my hour.

JOHN DRYDEN
TRANSLATED *from* HORACE'S ODES

D O NOT seek death. Death will find you, but seek the road which makes death a fulfilment . . . In the last analysis, it is our conception of death which decides our answers to all the questions that life puts to us.

DAG HAMMARSKJÖLD, from MARKINGS

O UR CRITICAL day is not the very day of our death; but the whole course of our life.

JOHN DONNE

WHEN RABBI Bunam was lying on his deathbed, he said to his wife, who was weeping bitterly, 'Why do you weep? All my life has been given to me merely that I might learn to die.'

CHASIDIC

WHEN WE are dead, and people weep for us and grieve, let it be because we touched their lives with beauty and simplicity. Let it not be said that life was good to us, but, rather, that we were good to life.

JACOB P. RUDIN

A MAN'S TRUE wealth is the good he does in this world.

ISLAM: HADITH OF MUSLIM

To REFRAIN from evil, to achieve good, to purify one's mind – this is the teaching of the Buddhas.

BUDDHISM: DHAMMAPADA 183

BIRTH DOES not lead to greatness; but the cultivation of virtues by a person leads him to greatness.

JAINISM: VAJJALAGAM 687

THE LIGHT of a good character surpasseth the light of the sun and the radiance thereof. Whoso attaineth unto it is accounted as a jewel among men.

BAHÁ'Í FAITH: TABLETS OF BAHÁ'U'LLÁH 36

THE SUPERIOR man, seeing what is good, imitates it; Seeing what is bad, he corrects it in himself.

CONFUCIANISM: I CHING 42; GAIN

THIS WORLD is like a vestibule before the World to Come; prepare yourself in the vestibule that you may enter the hall.

JUDAISM: MISHNAH, ABOTH 4,21

TO BE what we are, and to become what we are capable of becoming, is the only end of life.

R. L. STEVENSON, *from* FAMILIAR STUDIES OF MEN AND BOOKS

BEYOND DEATH

Peace, peace! he is not dead, he doth not sleep –
He hath awakened from the dream of life.

PERCY BYSSHE SHELLEY

I AM STANDING upon that foreshore. A ship at my side spreads her white sails to the morning breeze and starts for the blue ocean. She is an object of beauty and strength and I stand and watch her until at length she hangs like a speck of white cloud just where the sea and sky come down to mingle with each other. Then someone at my side says, 'There! She's gone!' 'Gone where?' 'Gone from my sight, that's all'. She is just as large in mast and spar and hull as ever she was when she left my side; just as able to bear her load of living freight to the place of her destination. Her diminished size is in me, not in her. And just at that moment when someone at my side says, 'There! She's gone!' there are other eyes watching her coming and other voices ready to take up the glad shout, 'Here she comes!' And that is dying.

VICTOR HUGO, *from* TOILERS OF THE SEA

WHEN YOU take the wires of the cage apart, you do not hurt the bird, but you help it. You let it out of its prison. How do you know that death does not help me when it takes the wires of my cage down? – that it does not release me, and put me in some better place and better condition of life?

BISHOP RANDOLPH S. FOSTER

UP-HILL

Does the road wind up-hill all the way?
    Yes, to the very end.
Will the day's journey take the whole long day?
    From morn to night, my friend.

But is there for the night a resting-place?
    A roof for when the slow dark hours begin.
May not the darkness hide it from my face?
    You cannot miss that inn.

Shall I meet other wayfarers at night?
    Those who have gone before.
Then must I knock, or call when just in sight?
    They will not keep you standing at that door.

Shall I find comfort, travel-sore and weak?
    Of labour you shall find the sum.
Will there be beds for me and all who seek?
    Yes, beds for all who come.

CHRISTINA ROSSETTI

THE NOBLE Soul in old age returns to God as to that port whence she set forth on the sea of this life. And as the good mariner, when he approaches port, furls his sails . . . so should we furl the sails of our worldly affairs and turn to God with our whole mind and heart, so that we may arrive at that port with all sweetness and peace.

DANTE, *from* CONVIVIO

LOVE IS life. All, all that I understand, I understand only because I love. All is, all exists only because I love. All is bound up in love alone. Love is God, and dying means for me a particle of love, to go back to the universal and eternal source of love.

LEO TOLSTOY, *from* WAR AND PEACE

SONNET X

DEATH BE not proud, though some have called thee
Mighty and dreadful, for thou art not so,
For those, whom thou think'st thou dost overthrow,
Die not, poor death, nor yet canst thou kill me;
From rest and sleep, which but thy pictures be,
Much pleasure, then from thee, much more must flow,
And soonest our best men with thee do go,
Rest of their bones, and souls delivery.
Thou art slave to Fate, chance, kings, and desperate men,
And dost with poison, war, and sickness dwell,
And poppy, or charms can make us sleep as well,
And better than thy stroke; why swell'st thou then?
One short sleep past, we wake eternally,
And death shall be no more, death, thou shalt die.

JOHN DONNE

Hᴏᴡ ᴅᴏ I know the love of life is not a delusion; and that the dislike of death is not like a child that is lost and does not know the way home?

Tᴀᴏɪsᴍ: Cʜᴜᴀɴɢ-ᴛᴢᴜ

As ʀɪᴠᴇʀs flow into the sea and in so doing lose name and form, even so the wise man, freed from name and form, attains the Supreme Being, the Self-luminous, the Infinite.

Hɪɴᴅᴜɪsᴍ: Mᴜɴᴅᴀᴋᴀ Uᴘᴀɴɪsʜᴀᴅ

Tʜᴇ ʙᴏᴅʏ dies but the spirit is not entombed.

Bᴜᴅᴅʜɪsᴍ: Dʜᴀᴍᴍᴀᴘᴀᴅᴀ 151

Sᴏᴍᴇᴏɴᴇ ᴀsᴋᴇᴅ: 'How will I reach you?' 'Leave your body behind and approach,' He answered.

Sᴜғɪsᴍ: Rūᴍī

AFTER ATTAINING its new condition the soul is grateful, for it has been released from the bondage of the limited to enjoy the liberties of the unlimited. It has been freed from a world of sorrow, grief and trials to live in a world of unending bliss and joy. The phenomenal and physical have been abandoned in order that it may attain the opportunities of the ideal and spiritual. Therefore, the souls of those who have passed away from earth and completed their span of mortal pilgrimage . . . have hastened to a world superior to this. They have soared away from these conditions of darkness and dim vision into the realm of light. These are the only considerations which can comfort and console those whom they leave behind.

BAHÁ'Í FAITH: 'ABDU'L-BAHÁ

WHAT, I pray you, is dying? Just what it is to put off a garment. For the body is about the soul as a garment; and after laying this aside for a short time by means of death, we shall resume it again with the more splendour.

CHRISTIANITY: ST JOHN CHRYSOSTOM

DEATH SHALL HAVE NO DOMINION

AND DEATH shall have no dominion.
Dead men naked they shall be one
With the man in the wind and the west moon;
When their bones are picked clean and the clean bones gone,
They shall have stars at elbow and foot;
Though they go mad they shall be sane,
Though they sink through the sea they shall rise again;
Though lovers be lost love shall not;
And death shall have no dominion.

And death shall have no dominion.
Under the windings of the sea
They lying long shall not die windily;
Twisting on racks when sinews give way,
Strapped to a wheel, yet they shall not break;
Faith in their hands shall snap in two,
And the unicorn evils run them through;
Split all ends up they shan't crack;
And death shall have no dominion.

And death shall have no dominion
No more may gulls cry at their ears
Or waves break loud on the seashores;
Where blew a flower may a flower no more
Lift its head to the blows of the rain;
Though they be mad and dead as nails,
Heads of the characters hammer through daisies;
Break in the sun till the sun breaks down,
And death shall have no dominion.

DYLAN THOMAS

TELL ME, my soul, can this be Death?
The world recedes; it disappears!
Heaven opens on my eyes! my ears
With sounds seraphic ring.
Lend, lend your wings! I mount! I fly!
O Grave! where is thy victory?
O Death! where is thy sting!

ALEXANDER POPE, *from* THE DYING CHRISTIAN TO HIS SOUL

WE SEEM to give them back to thee, O God, who gavest them to us. Yet, as thou didst not lose them in giving, so do we not lose them by their return. Not as the world giveth, givest thou, O lover of souls. What thou givest, thou takest not away, for what is thine is ours also, if we are thine. And life is eternal and love is immortal, and death is only an horizon, and an horizon is nothing save the limit of our sight. Lift us up, strong son of God, that we may see further: cleanse our eyes that we may see more clearly: draw us closer to thyself that we may know ourselves to be nearer to our loved ones who are with thee. And while thou dost prepare a place for us, prepare us also for that happy place, that where thou art, we may be also for evermore.

WILLIAM PENN, *from* FRUITS OF SOLITUDE

THAT DAY, which you fear as being the end of all things, is the birthday of your eternity.

SENECA, *from* MORAL AND POLITICAL ESSAYS

THE WORLD is not conclusion;
　　A sequel stands beyond,
Invisible, as music,
　　But positive, as sound.
It beckons and it baffles;
　　Philosophies don't know,
And through a riddle, at the last,
　　Sagacity must go.
To guess it puzzles scholars;
　　To gain it, men have shown
Contempt of generations,
　　And crucifixion known.

EMILY DICKINSON

THE MEANING of death is not the annihilation of the spirit, but its separation from the body, and that the resurrection and day of assembly do not mean a return to a new existence after annihilation, but the bestowal of a new form or frame to the spirit.

AL-GHAZZÁLÍ, *from* ALCHEMY OF HAPPINESS

I USED to think,
Loving life so greatly,
That to die would be
Like leaving a party
Before the end.
Now I know that the party
Is really happening
Somewhere else;
That the light and the music –
Escaping in snatches
To make the pulse beat
And the tempo quicken –
Come from a long way away.
And I know, too,
That when I get there
The music will never
End.

ANON

DO NOT MOURN
FOR ME

I can't think of a more wonderful thanksgiving for the life I have had than that everyone should be jolly at my funeral.

LORD LOUIS MOUNTBATTEN

REGRET NOT ME

Regret not me;
Beneath the sunny tree
I lie uncaring, slumbering peacefully.
Swift as the light
I flew my faery flight;
Ecstatically I moved, and feared no night.
I did not know
That heydays fade and go.
But deemed that what was would be always so.
I skipped at morn
Between the yellowing corn,
Thinking it good and glorious to be born.
I ran at eves
Among the piled-up sheaves,
Dreaming, 'I grieve not, therefore nothing grieves.'
Now soon will come
The apple, pear, and plum,
And hinds will sing, and autumn insects hum.

Again you will fare
To cider-makings rare,
And junketings; but I shall not be there.
Yet gaily sing
Until the pewter ring
Those songs we sang when we went gipsying.
And lightly dance
Some triple-timed romance
In coupled figures, and forget mischance;
And mourn not me
Beneath the yellowing tree;
For I shall mind not, slumbering peacefully.

THOMAS HARDY

No Mourning, By Request

COME NOT to mourn for me with solemn tread
Clad in dull weeds of sad and sable hue,
Nor weep because my tale of life's told through,
Casting light dust on my untroubled head.
Nor linger near me while the sexton fills
My grave with earth – but go gay-garlanded,
And in your halls a shining banquet spread
And gild your chambers o'er with daffodils.

Fill your tall goblets with white wine and red,
And sing brave songs of gallant love and true,
Wearing soft robes of emerald and blue,
And dance, as I your dances oft have led,
And laugh, as I have often laughed with you –
And be most merry – after I am dead.

WINIFRED HOLTBY

Do NOT stand at my grave and weep.
I am not there, I do not sleep.
I am a thousand winds that blow.
I am diamond glints on snow.
I am the sunlight on ripened grain.
I am the gentle autumn rain.
When you awaken in the morning's hush,
I am the swift uplifting rush
Of quiet birds in circled flight.
I am the soft stars that shine at night.
Do not stand at my grave and cry,
I am not there; I did not die.

ANON

ON THE day of death, when my bier is on the move, do not suppose that I have any pain at leaving this world.

Do not weep for me, say not 'Alas, alas!' You will fall into the devil's snare – that would indeed be alas!

When you see my hearse, say not 'Parting, parting!' That time there will be for me union and encounter.

When you commit me to the grave, say not 'Farewell, farewell!' For the grave is a veil over the reunion of paradise.

Having seen the going-down, look upon the coming-up; how should setting impair the sun and the moon?

To you it appears as setting, but it is a rising; the tomb appears as a prison, but it is release for the soul.

What seed ever went down into the earth which did not grow? Why do you doubt so regarding the human seed?

What bucket ever went down and came not out full? Why this complaining of the well by the Joseph of the spirit?

When you have closed your mouth on this side, open it on that, for your shout of triumph will echo in the placeless air.

RŪMĪ

SONG

WHEN I am dead, my dearest,
    Sing no sad songs for me;
Plant thou no roses at my head,
    Nor shady cypress tree:
Be the green grass above me
    With showers and dewdrops wet;
And if thou wilt, remember,
    And if thou wilt, forget.

I shall not see the shadows,
    I shall not feel the rain;
I shall not hear the nightingale
    Sing on, as if in pain:
And dreaming through the twilight
    That doth not rise nor set,
Haply I may remember,
    And haply may forget.

CHRISTINA ROSSETTI

CROSSING THE BAR

SUNSET AND evening star,
    And one clear call for me!
And may there be no moaning of the bar,
    When I put out to sea,

But such a tide as moving seems asleep,
    Too full for sound and foam
When that which drew from out the boundless deep
    Turns again home.

Twilight and evening bell,
    And after that the dark!
And may there be no sadness of farewell,
    When I embark;

For tho' from out our bourne of Time and Place
    The flood may bear me far,
I hope to see my Pilot face to face
    When I have crost the bar.

ALFRED, LORD TENNYSON

WHEN I must leave you for a while,
Please do not grieve and shed wild tears
And hug your sorrow to you through the years
But start out bravely with a gallant smile;
And for my sake and in my name
Live on and do all things the same.
Feed not your loneliness on empty days,
But fill each waking hour in useful ways.
Reach out your hand in comfort and hold me dear,
And I in turn will comfort you and hold you near,
And never, never be afraid to die,
For I am waiting for you in the sky!

ANON

WHEN CHUANG Tzu's wife died, Hui Tzu came to the house to join in the rites of mourning. To his surprise he found Chuang Tzu sitting with an inverted bowl on his knees, drumming upon it and singing a song. 'After all,' said Hui Tzu, 'she lived with you, brought up your children, grew old along with you. That you should not mourn for her is bad enough; but to let your friends find you drumming and singing – that is going too far!' 'You misjudge me,' said Chuang Tzu. 'When she died, I was in despair, as any man might well be. But soon, pondering on what had happened, I told myself that in death no strange new fate befalls us . . .

Life in its turn has evolved death. For not nature only but man's being has its seasons, its sequence of spring and autumn, summer and winter. If someone is tired and has gone to lie down, we do not pursue him with shouting and bawling. She whom I have lost has lain down to sleep for a while in the Great Inner Room. To break in upon her rest with the noise of lamentation would but show that I knew nothing of nature's Sovereign Law.

CHUANG-TZU, *from* A. WALEY, THREE WAYS OF THOUGHT

IF I SHOULD die and leave you here awhile,
Be not like others, sore undone, who keep
Long vigils by the silent dust and weep.
For my sake turn again to life and smile,
Nerving thy heart and trembling hand to do
Something to comfort weaker hearts than thine.
Complete these dear unfinished tasks of mine,
And I, perchance, may therein comfort you!

A. PRICE HUGHES

IF I SHOULD go before the rest of you
Break not a flower or inscribe a stone,
Nor when I'm gone speak in a Sunday voice
But be the usual selves that I have known.
Weep if you must,
Parting is hell,
But life goes on
So sing as well.

JOYCE GRENFELL, *from* JOYCE BY HERSELF AND HER FRIENDS

COMFORT AND CONSOLATION

Earth has no sorrow

That heaven cannot heal.

Sir Thomas More

G RIEF IS a fruit; God does not make it grow upon a branch too feeble to bear it.

VICTOR HUGO

I WRITE TO you because every expression of human sympathy brings some little comfort, if it be only to remind such as you that you are not alone in the world. I know nothing can make up for such a loss as yours. But you will still have love on earth all round you; and *his* love is not dead. It lives still in the next world for you, and perhaps with you. For why should not those who are gone, if they are gone to their Lord, be actually nearer us, not further from us, in the heavenly world, praying for us, and it may be influencing and guiding us in a hundred ways, of which we in our prison-house of mortality cannot dream.

CHARLES KINGSLEY

GRIEVE NOT; though the journey of life be bitter, and the end unseen, there is no road which does not lead to an end.

HAFIZ, *from* THE DIVAN

AND THIS word: *Thou shalt be overcome*, was said full clearly and full mightily, for assuredness and comfort against all tribulations that may come. He said not: *Thou shalt not be tempested, thou shalt not be travailed, thou shalt not be afflicted*; but He said: *Thou shalt not be overcome*. God willeth that we take heed to these words, and that we be ever strong in sure trust, in weal and woe. For He loveth and enjoyeth us, and so willeth He that we love and enjoy Him and mightily trust in Him; and *all shall be well*.

JULIAN OF NORWICH, *from* REVELATIONS OF DIVINE LOVE

PUT FORTH thy leaf, thou lofty plane,
East wind and frost are safely gone;
With zephyr mild and balmy rain
The summer comes serenely on;
Earth, air, and sun and skies combine
To promise all that's kind and fair: –
But thou, O human heart of mine,
Be still, contain thyself, and bear.

December days were brief and chill,
The winds of March were wild and drear,
And, nearing and receding still,
Spring never would, we thought, be here.
The leaves that burst, the suns that shine,
Had, not the less, their certain date: –
And thou, O human heart of mine,
Be still, refrain thyself, and wait.

ARTHUR HUGH CLOUGH

NEVER SAY about anything, 'I have lost it,' but only 'I have given it back.' Is your child dead? It has been given back. Is your wife dead? She has been returned.

EPICTETUS, from DISCOURSES

ONLY FAITH in a life after death, in a brighter world where dear ones will meet again – only that and the measured tramp of time can give consolation.

WINSTON CHURCHILL

Psalm 23

THE LORD is my shepherd, I shall not want.
    He maketh me to lie down in green pastures,
he leadeth me beside the still waters,
    he restoreth my soul.
He leadeth my in the paths of righteousness
    for his name's sake.
Even though I walk
    through the valley of the shadow of death,
I will fear no evil:
    for thou art with me;
thy rod and thy staff they comfort me.

Thou preparest a table before me
    in the presence of mine enemies:
thou anointest my head with oil;
    my cup runneth over.
Surely goodness and mercy shall follow me
    all the days of my life:
and I will dwell in the house of the LORD
    for ever.

THERE IS no flock, however watched and tended,
    But one dead lamb is there!
There is no fireside, howsoe'er defended,
    But has one vacant chair!

The air is full of farewells to the dying,
    And mournings for the dead;
The heart of Rachel for her children crying,
    Will not be comforted!

Let us be patient! These severe afflictions
    Not from the ground arise,
But oftentimes celestial benedictions
    Assume this dark disguise.

We see but dimly through the mists and vapours;
    Amid these earthly damps,
What seem to us but sad, funereal tapers
    May be heaven's distant lamps.

There is no Death! What seems so is transition;
    This life of mortal breath
Is but a suburb of the life elysian,
    Whose portal we call Death.

HENRY WADSWORTH LONGFELLOW, *from* RESIGNATION

ON ANOTHER'S SORROW

CAN I see another's woe,
And not be in sorrow too?
Can I see another's grief,
And not seek for kind relief?

Can I see a falling tear,
And not feel my sorrow's share?
Can a father see his child
Weep, nor be with sorrow fill'd?

Can a mother sit and hear
An infant groan an infant fear?
No, no! never can it be!
Never, never can it be!

And can He who smiles on all
Hear the wren with sorrows small,
Hear the small bird's grief and care,
Hear the woes that infants bear,

And not sit beside the nest,
Pouring pity in their breast;
And not sit the cradle near,
Weeping tear on infant's tear;

And not sit both night and day,
Wiping all our tears away?
O, no! never can it be!
Never, never can it be!

He doth give His joy to all;
He becomes an infant small;
He becomes a man of woe;
He doth feel the sorrow too.

Think not thou canst sigh a sigh,
And thy Maker is not by;
Think not thou canst weep a tear
And thy Maker is not near.

O! He gives to us his joy
That our grief He may destroy;
Till our grief is fled and gone
He doth sit by us and moan.

WILLIAM BLAKE

THE PILLAR OF THE CLOUD

LEAD, KINDLY Light, amid the encircling gloom,
    Lead Thou me on!
The night is dark, and I am far from home –
    Lead Thou me on!
Keep Thou my feet; I do not ask to see
The distant scene – one step enough for me.

I was not ever thus, nor pray'd that Thou
    Shouldst lead me on.
I loved to choose and see my path, but now
    Lead Thou me on!
I loved the garish day, and, spite of fears,
Pride ruled my will: remember not past years.

So long Thy power hath blest me, sure it still
    Will lead me on
O'er moor and fen, o'er crag and torrent, till
    The night is gone;
And with the morn those angel faces smile
Which I have loved long since, and lost awhile.

JOHN HENRY NEWMAN

SAVE ME, O God,
    for the waters have come up to my neck.
I sink in the miry depths,
    where there is no foothold.
I have come into the deep waters;
    the floods engulf me.
I am worn out calling for help;
    my throat is parched.
My eyes fail,
    looking for my God . . .
But I pray to you, O LORD,
    in the time of your favour;
in your great love, O God,
    answer me with your sure salvation . . .
Do not let the floodwaters engulf me
    or the depths swallow me up
    or the pit close its mouth over me.
Answer me, O LORD, out of the goodness of your love;
    in your great mercy turn to me.
Do not hide your face from your servant;
    answer me quickly for I am in trouble.

From PSALM 69

Comfort and Consolation ❧ 101

SONG

LIFE IS ours in vain
Lacking love, which never
Counts the loss or gain.
But remember, ever
Love is linked with pain.

Light and sister shade
Shape each mortal morrow
Seek not to evade
Love's companion Sorrow,
and be not dismayed.

Grief is not in vain,
It's for our completeness.
If the fates ordain
Love to bring life's sweetness,
Welcome too its pain.

KATH WALKER

A NEW BEGINNING

Let mourning stop when one's grief is fully expressed.

CICERO

FOR YOU,
Let the dreams that are gone sleep fast my love,
Let the tears and fears of yesterday's storm,
For the darkness you saw is past my love,
So smile and a new day is born.
The seasons of life will go on my love,
And the sails of your ship may be torn,
But the secrets beneath your feet my love,
Are the flowers that are yet to be born.
Let the tears that you shed fall sweet my love,
For the pain goes and rainbows come without warning.
All the seasons will surely return my love
And new life will be born in the dawning.

ANON

WITH YOU a part of me hath passed away;
For in the peopled forest of my mind
A tree made leafless by this wintry wind
Shall never don again its green array.
Chapel and fireside, country road and bay,
Have something of their friendliness resigned;
Another, if I would, I could not find,
And I am grown much older in a day.
But yet I treasure in my memory
Your gift of charity, and young heart's ease,
And the dear honour of your amity;
For these once mine, my life is rich with these.
And I scarce know which part may greater be –
What I keep of you, or you rob from me.

GEORGE SANTAYANA

W<small>E ALL</small> live together, and those of us who love and know, live so most. We help each other – even unconsciously, each in our own effort, we lighten the effort of others, we contribute to the sum of success, make it possible for others to live. Sorrow comes in great waves – no one can know that better than you – but it rolls over us, and though it may almost smother us it leaves us on the spot, and we know that if it is strong we are stronger, inasmuch as it passes and we remain. It wears us, uses us, but we wear it and use it in return; and it is blind, whereas we after a manner see.

H<small>ENRY</small> J<small>AMES</small>

JULIAN GRENFELL

BECAUSE OF you we will be glad and gay,
Remembering you, we may be brave and strong;
And hail the advent of each dangerous day,
And meet the last adventure with a song.

And, as you proudly gave your jewelled gift,
We'll give our lesser offering with a smile,
Nor falter on the path where, all too swift,
You led the way and leapt the golden stile.

Whether new paths, new heights to climb, you find,
Or gallop through the unfooted asphodel,
We know you know we shall not lag behind,
Nor halt to waste a moment on a fear;
And you will speed us onward with a cheer,
And wave beyond the stars that all is well.

MAURICE BARING

THEN, SING ye birds, sing, sing a joyous song!
    And let the young lambs bound
    As to the tabor's sound!
We in thought will join your throng,
    Ye that pipe and ye that play,
    Ye that through your hearts to-day
    Feel the gladness of the May!
What though the radiance which was once so bright
Be now for ever taken from my sight,
    Though nothing can bring back the hour
Of splendour in the grass, of glory in the flower,
    We will grieve not, rather find
    Strength in what remains behind –
    In the primal sympathy
    Which having been must ever be,
    In the soothing thoughts that spring
    Out of all human suffering,
    In the faith that looks through death,
In years that bring the philosophic mind.

WILLIAM WORDSWORTH, *from* INTIMATIONS OF IMMORTALITY

DEATH CLOSES all: but something ere the end,
Some work of noble note, may yet be done,
Not unbecoming men that strove with Gods.
The lights begin to twinkle from the rocks:
The long day wanes; the slow moon climbs: the deep
Moans round with many voices. Come, my friends,
'Tis not too late to seek a newer world.
Push off, and sitting well in order smite
The sounding furrows; for my purpose holds
To sail beyond the sunset, and the baths
Of all the western stars, until I die.
It may be that the gulfs will wash us down:
It may be we shall touch the Happy Isles,
And see the great Achilles, whom we knew.
Tho' much is taken, much abides; and tho'
We are not now that strength which in old days
Moved earth and heaven; that which we are, we are;
One equal temper of heroic hearts,
Made weak by time and fate, but strong in will
To strive, to seek, to find, and not to yield.

ALFRED, LORD TENNYSON

STRENGTH

INSIDE,
I am making myself strong.
I am weaving bands of steel
To bind my soul.
I am knitting stitches of suffering
Into my hands
To make them strong.
I am strengthening my mind
With the warp and the weft
Of weariness and endurance.
I am binding my faith
With the bonds of psalms and songs
Of all who have suffered.
In time,
I will be tempered like fine steel
To bend, but not to break.

MARJORIE PIZER

DEEP SOBS –

that start beneath my heart
and hold my body in a grip that hurts.
The lump that swells inside my throat
brings pain that tries to choke.
Then tears course down my cheeks –
I drop my head in my so empty hands
abandoning myself to deep dark grief
and know that with the passing time
will come relief.
That though the pain may stay
There soon will come a day
When I can say her name
and be at peace.

NORAH LENEY

IT IS better to grieve than not to grieve. Grief at least tells me that I was not always what I am now. I was once selected for happiness – let the memory of that abide by me. You pass by an old ruined house in a desolate land & do not heed it – but if you hear that that house is haunted by a wild & beautiful spirit, it acquires an interest & beauty of its own.

MARY SHELLEY, *from* JOURNALS

PRAYERS FROM AROUND THE WORLD

More things are wrought by prayer
Than this world dreams of.

ALFRED, LORD TENNYSON

PRAYERS FOR COMFORT AND CONSOLATION

SUPPORT US, Lord, when we are silent through grief! Comfort us when we are bent down with sorrow! Help us as we bear the weight of our loss! Lord, our Rock and our Redeemer, give us strength!

JUDAISM: FUNERAL SERVICE

O GOD, GIVE me light in my heart and light in my tongue and light in my hearing and light in my sight and light in my feeling and light in all my body and light before me and light behind me. Give me, I pray Thee, light on my right hand and light on my left hand and light above me and light beneath me, O Lord, increase light within me and give me light to illuminate me.

ISLAM: ASCRIBED TO MUHAMMAD

LORD, MAKE me a channel of Thy peace; where there is hatred may I bring love; where there is injury, pardon; where there is doubt, faith; where there is despair, hope; where there is darkness, light; and where there is sadness, joy. O Divine Lover, grant that we may not so much seek to be consoled as to console; to be understood as to understand; to be loved as to love; for it is in giving that we receive, it is in pardoning that we are pardoned, and it is in dying that we are born to eternal life.

CHRISTIANITY: ST FRANCIS OF ASSISI

HE WHO calls to God from the depths of his heart, will find his abode in the clear skies of love.

SUFISM: ALI NADER

WA-KON'DA,
here needy he stands,
and I am he.

OUR FATHER the Sky, hear us and make us bold.
O Our Mother the earth, hear us and give us support.
O Spirit of the East, send us your wisdom.
O Spirit of the South, may we walk your path of life.
O Spirit of the West, may we always be ready for the long
    journey.
O Spirit of the North, purify us with your cleansing winds.

REVERENCING THE Buddha, we offer flowers:
Flowers that today are fresh and sweetly blooming,
Flowers that tomorrow are faded and fallen.
Our bodies too, like flowers, will pass away.

Reverencing the Buddha, we offer candles.
To Him who is the Light, we offer light.
From His greater lamp a lesser lamp we light within us,
The lamp of wisdom shining within our hearts.

Reverencing the Buddha, we offer incense,
Incense whose fragrance pervades the air,
The fragrance of the perfect life, sweeter than incense,
Spreads in all directions throughout the world.

BUDDHISM

O GOD! REFRESH and gladden my spirit. Purify my heart. Illumine my mind. I lay all my affairs in Thy hand. Thou art my Guide and my Refuge. I will no longer be sorrowful and grieved; I will be a happy and joyful being. O God! I will no longer be full of anxiety, nor will I let trouble harass me. I will not dwell on the unpleasant things of life. O God! Thou art kinder to me than I am to myself. I dedicate myself to Thee, O Lord.

BAHÁ'Í FAITH: 'ABDU'L BAHÁ

BESTOW, O GOD, this grace upon us, that in the school of suffering we should learn self-conquest, and through sorrow, even if it be against our will, learn self-control.

AESCHYLUS

THE LORD bless you
  and keep you;
the Lord make his face shine upon you
  and be gracious to you;
the Lord turn his face upon you
  and give you peace.

JUDAISM: NUMBERS 6:24–6

O GOD, THE Strength of the weak, the Comfort of the sorrowful, the Friend of the lonely: let not sorrow overwhelm Thy children, nor anguish of heart turn them from Thee. Grant that in the patience of hope and the fellowship of Christ they may continue in Thy service and in all godly living, until at length they also attain unto fullness of life before Thy face, through Jesus Christ our Lord.

CHRISTIANITY: METHODIST BOOK OF OFFICES

ALL THINGS pass
A sunrise does not last all morning
All things pass
A cloudburst does not last all day
All things pass
Nor a sunset all night
All things pass
What always changes?

Earth . . . sky . . . thunder . . .
    mountain . . . water . . .
    wind . . . fire . . . lake . . .

These change
And if these do not last

Do man's visions last?
Do man's illusions?

Take things as they come

All things pass

TAOISM: LAO-TZU

MAY THERE be peace in the higher regions;
May there be peace in the firmament;
May there be peace on earth.

May the waters flow peacefully;
May the herbs and plants grow peacefully;
May all the divine powers bring unto us peace.

The supreme Lord is peace.
May we all be in peace, peace and only peace;
And may that peace come unto each of us.

Shanti! Shanti! Shanti!

HINDUISM: THE VEDAS

IN THE rising of the sun and in its going down,
  we remember them.
In the blowing of the wind and in the chill of winter,
  We remember them.
In the opening of buds and in the rebirth of spring,
  we remember them.
In the blueness of the sky and in the warmth of summer,
  we remember them.
In the rustling of leaves and in the beauty of autumn,
  we remember them.
In the beginning of the year and when it ends,
  we remember them.
When we are weary and in need of strength,
  we remember them.
When we are lost and sick at heart,
  we remember them.
When we have joys we yearn to share,
  we remember them.
So long as we live, they too shall live,
  for they are now a part of us, as
  we remember them.

JUDAISM

PRAYERS FOR THE DEPARTED

O MY GOD! O Thou forgiver of sins! Bestower of gifts! Dispeller of afflictions!

Verily, I beseech Thee to forgive the sins of such as have abandoned the physical garment and ascended to the spiritual world.

O my Lord! Purify them from trespasses, dispel their sorrows, and change their darkness into light. Cause them to enter the garden of happiness, cleanse them with the most pure water, and grant them to behold Thy splendours on the loftiest mount.

BAHÁ'Í FAITH: 'ABDU'L-BAHÁ

GIVE THEM rest with the devout and the just, in the place of the pasture of rest and of refreshment, of waters in the paradise of delight; whence grief and pain and sighing have fled away.

CHRISTIANITY: EARLY PRAYER

HE HAS shed his frail earthly mansion and departed this life to live hereafter in the realm of the spirit. His earthly work is done and he has laid down his burden. From the din and dust of life's struggle, he has gone to the deathless world of peace and rest where light fades not and happiness fails not. Our beloved has died in body to live in spirit a life higher and nobler than our thoughts can measure and minds can conceive. Let him rest in everlasting peace and joy with Thee, Ahura Mazda.

ZOROASTRIANISM

Thou goest home this night to thy home of winter,
To thy home of autumn, of spring, and of summer;
Thou goest home this night to thy perpetual home,
To thine eternal bed, to thine eternal slumber.

    Sleep thou, sleep, and away with thy sorrow,
    Sleep thou, sleep, and away with thy sorrow,
    Sleep thou, sleep, and away with thy sorrow;
    Sleep thou, beloved, in the Rock of the fold . . .

The shade of death lies upon thy face, beloved,
But the Jesus of grace has His hand round about thee;
    In nearness to the Trinity farewell to thy pains,
Christ stands before thee and peace is in His mind . . .

Sleep, O sleep in the calm of all calm,
Sleep, O sleep in the guidance of guidance,
Sleep, O sleep in the love of all loves,
    Sleep, O beloved, in the Lord of life,
    Sleep, O beloved, in the God of life!

NINETEENTH-CENTURY CELTIC ORAL TRADITION

Acknowledgements

• Twelve Songs: 'IX'. Copyright © The Estate of W. H. Auden, 1991. By permission of Faber and Faber. • 'Julian Grenfell'. By permission of A. P. Watt Ltd on behalf of The Trustees of the Maurice Baring Trust. • 'For the Fallen (September 1914)'. By permission of the Society of Authors on behalf of the Lawrence Binyon Estate. • *The Meditations of Marcus Aurelius*, translated by A. S. L. Farquharson, OUP, 1944. By permission of Oxford University Press. • 'Do Not Mourn for Me'. Copyright © The Joyce Grenfell Memorial Trust, 1980. By permission of Macmillan Publishers Ltd. • from *Markings*, Dag Hammarskjöld. By permission of Faber and Faber. • 'Regret Not Me', Thomas Hardy. Copyright © Samuel Hynes, 1984. By permission of Macmillan Publishers Ltd. • 'Words About Grief' and 'For a Child Born Dead'. Copyright © Elizabeth Jennings, 1982. By permission of David Higham Associates. • Excerpt from *The Modern Temper*. Copyright © 1929 by Harcourt Brace & Company and renewed 1956 by Joseph Wood Krutch, reprinted by permission of the publisher. • *A Grief Observed*. Copyright © Clive Staples Lewis, 1961. By permission of Faber and Faber. • Your Head in Mine, 1994. Copyright © The Estate of Sasha Moorsom, 1994. By permission of David Higham Associates. • 'Strength', from *To You the Living, poems of bereavement and loss*, Pinchgut Press, 6 Oaks Avenue, NSW, Australia. Copyright © Marjorie Pizer, 1973. By permission of Marjorie Pizer. • 'Up-Hill' and 'Song', Christina Rossetti. By permission of Louisiana State University Press. • 'Eurydice', Edith Sitwell. By permission of David Higham Associates. • 'And Death Shall Have No Dominion', Dylan Thomas. By permission of David Higham Associates. • 'Song' from *The Dawn is at Hand*. Copyright © Kath Walker, 1992. By permission of Marion Boyars Publishers, London, New York.

INDEX OF AUTHORS AND SOURCES